# Onshore Winds

# Onshore Winds

## a collection of poetry

*Peter Cunliffe*

First Published in 2024 by Kindle | Direct Publishing

ISBN: 9798335017152

For: Susanne, Kelsie and Corrinne,
daughters who joined our family,
and the blessing of grandchildren on three continents
Bobbi, Rupert;
Ezra, Zoe, Frankie Bea, Alana;
Ayla, Talley and Kian

# Onshore Winds

## Contents

# Preface and Acknowledgements

The powerlessness and grief felt during the early months of the Covid lockdowns in the United Kingdom found its expression in me through poetic writing, and sharing this in my ministry as a parish priest in Hemingford Grey.  Reciting poetry in public worship was a means of expressing these deeply held emotions and as a means of prayer. Very often it was sharing and responding to parishioners life experiences; and it was they who encouraged me to publish my first collection of poetry, 'The North Winds Blow'[1].

Continuing to put pencil to paper as I approached retirement and subsequently joining a new parish with a license to officiate, has been cathartic.

Indeed moving away from the Cambridgeshire village, which has been our home and ministry for over 20 years - relationships, familiar places, roles and responsibilities is a brutal dislocation.

The journey to our new home in West Sussex, continues to be one of rediscovery. Being close to the sea it is subject to blustery onshore winds, providing a connection with my first collection of poetry.  While life goes on in the ordinary everyday, sometimes filled with beauty and joy, and at others

_____

[1] Available on Amazon

with pain and ugliness, I continue to find pencil and paper a means for expression and theological reflection.

Practicing stillness, listening and reflecting on the presence of God in the ordinary and in Holy Scripture is borne out in these written words. A walk to the shoreline in my NorthFace or shirt sleeves, watching the birds and the tides whatever the weather, is a reminder of the One who prevails.

I offer this second collection trusting that some words resonate with the reader's experience and bring you words of light and hope.

Peter Cunliffe, Spring 2024

# Life and Birth

Grandchildren are a wonderful gift, as is the promise of God's faithfulness from generation to generation. Each grandchild brings their own unique character and that special connection is so much more than DNA.

As I enjoy my grandchildren, scattered around the globe, I am reminded (at the time of writing) of the pain of Palestinian grandfathers in Gaza and the West Bank, and pray with the Palestinian Church for the coming of Yeshua, the Prince of Peace.

*After chatting with two-year old granddaughter on a video call.*

## Frankie Bea

I held my breath while you came
your bright eyes meeting your mother's
soft slumbering in your father's arms
your brother's eye long-waiting filled with joy.

He held you precious gift of life
gazing in wonder at his little sister
open hands with tiny fingers talked
with expressive face and soon

You found your feet and walked
your voice came quickly adding sound to hands
delighting in the cat and dog
adventurous you climbed

So much you have to say if only
you could find those words, so
pulling, running, bundling your days and
in moments of stillness raptured

By living things that encroach your space
snake sliding, spiders dancing
curling toes in sand, hopping 'round jelly fish
yearning to ride the surf with brother, mom and dad

Calling again loud and lively as lorikeets
voice raised in laughter and giggles
open hands with tiny fingers talking
with expressive face and eyes.

*Two and a half.*

## Ayla

If the sun's not shining in San Clemente
Then you face is always alight
Wide eyes dancing with delight
Looking forward to going

Adventurous climbing in the play-park
Gazing out to sea while waiting turns
To slide the big blue spout then
Rushing about with sandy toes

Joy-spilling along the pier you go
Determined chasing after gulls
Widest smiles beaming
Ribboned bunches bouncing

'Round Papi's house you race
In circles on your bee
Snuggling tight on Bahti's sofa
On screen transfixed by favourite show

Oatley, family Maine Coon
Curled sleeping by your side
Serving ice-cream from the playhouse
A playful tug at faithful Rivi's coat[2]

Holding hands with Mom
You skip along the street
Held high in Daddy's arms
You lift your hand in praise.

---

[2] Rivi is a Burmese Mountain dog.

*Born 10th November, California*

## Talley

It was on the tenth Talley came, in the middle of our night

another November day to remember

Wide-eyed you gazed around, the beginning of the day

Your mom tired by giving birth

Early in the morning, on that Pacific shore[3]

You breathed your first breath

Proud father's beanie crowned his smile

Cradled by his hands, you lay close to his heart

Moma's lips and Daddy's dimpled chin

Fingers circled, eyes closed, peaceful face

Four proud grandparents

Your voice we wait to hear.

---

[3] Reference to the 'Pacific shore' may be found in the first collection

## Alana

We counted the weeks of your gestation

and called upon our Father in heaven

ev'ry moment in our hearts

the gift of life held

in secret place you formed

already fully known

while hidden from our view

we heard your heart beat

saw you through ultrasound

but today you came

we held you in our arms

close to our loved-filled hearts

God has heard and answered

the meaning of your name

Alana.

# Life and Death

## Mercy Spoke

With gentle voice Mercy spoke to me
on this anniversary of her daughter's birth
Her custom to remember with a gift
the gift of life which she bore
with a gift to God

The pain of loss surpassed by grace
she passed the crumpled envelope and quietly spoke
"I want no mention as I mark this day"

Mercy bowed her head in prayer
As on her shoulders I laid my hand
"Amen" and "Hallelujahs" she raised
Her face beaming with delight

The image of Jesus in her eyes
She passed from our morning Eucharistic feast
Into the brightness of the summer's day
Gentle breeze and river flowing by

We speak of angels unawares
Was this such a one?
No, 'twas Abiola's mother.

# When a family member dies in tragic circumstances

The call was hard to hear striking the heart
The cost of embracing, enfolding, uniting
Met by parting, unfolding, tearing, yet it is to be
In the twinkling an eye the great redemption revealed
To him who walked by faith and not by sight.

The quiet-spirited adventurous pastor touched many
Eyesight failing but seeing more
As closer to the Father he drew near
With liberating joy he would sing
Campfire songs and songs of glory

Abide with me fast falls the eventide
In cathedrals of trees he lifted up his praise
On mountains and under stars at home
Across lakes glinting in sunlight he paddled
At one with creation and Creator

Soft tender-hearted he held children on his knee
And with delight he played their games
His smile greeting saints in glory while tears filled our eyes
Prepared and ready to give account
Of grace given and freely received.

*Visiting Hilda for the first time after the pandemic and after her 100th birthday.*

## Upright and in elegance dressed

Greeted by bright eyes and name
Warm generous hospitality offered
Beaming face shining delight and embrace
"Tell me how's your wife?"

Walls covered with birthday cards
The Queen's standing by her chair
Faces of family near and far
Look on this graceful centenarian
Gazing out beyond her room

"I am confused sometimes you know"
Yet in these moments there is clarity
Playful swipe at the fly on my knee
A coy chuckle at her impertinence
With a dignity beyond a doubt

School friends memorial card
Brings melancholy moment
Of another centenarian life passed
A looking back over joy filled years
With school friends and carefree days

"Tell me" as she looks forwards
"About your boys and theirs."
Delighting in the youngest adventurers
In this gift of life on earth
An interest of a youthful mind

Once the farmer's wife with pastoral note
She connects as psalm is spoken
"The Lord's my Shepherd" in the darkest valley
Brings a tear of sadness and joy
A life well-lived and of life to come

Head bowed in prayer
She grips my hand thoughts too deep to know
Her "amen" comes from the heart
And smiles adorn her face
Knowing her call will not be long.

*Following the death of two parishioners in close succession.*

## Holding-hope

When time ends and the Presence comes near

It is but a revelation of mortality

As sadness grips my heart

Holding-hope comforts the pain of loss

The weight is heavy in limited vision

The word of promise lifts my spirit

To a greater glory's coming day


If I had not loved I would be less

Compassion the gift to embrace

The pain of another held by holding-hope

A burden shared and lifted

The dreams of tomorrow certain

Promises a King and a Kingdom

Whose greater glory we'll share

Now constrained by time it's the day
When holding-hope sustains a wearied soul
Committing saints whose days are done
The mercy of the Father reaches down
Blessing our days in tenderness
Shared in the tears of His Son
Creator word, the speaker of life.

# Life

## The Courts of Justice

Randomly selected we sat in rows

Background wall of indistinguishable voices

A hesitancy to speak

Roll call of names before video of instructions

Fifteen follow to the courtroom


Twelve names called we sit as jurors

The judge thanks us for our service

Crown Prosecutor opens the case

It's time to take a break

We file out and in as hours and days pass


To'ing and fro'ing of fact and fiction

One perspective and then another

Learnèd friends conferring

Defence statement enacted by lawyer and police officer

Neighbours in dispute bruised in body and soul

Forgiveness a foreign word unspoken

Twelve strangers deliberate

Question for the judge on one solitary word

Verdict based on that word alone

Law would have the penultimate say


Beneath a wig twice his age the judge asks

"Have you reached a verdict?"

"Yes, not guilty"

A final offer of reconciliation yet unspoken

Love your neighbour as yourself

## Waiting - a jurors day

Waiting

For a waking alarm

For the kettle to boil

On the railway platform

In the queue for coffee

For security checks

For the courtroom day to start

For the ushers call

For a legal conversation to end

For another call to court

In the sunny calm

For a storm that's coming

For weather and whether

*Determined, Maggie celebrates Christmas in spite of MND; she died a month later.*

## Christmas Eve

Life spiralling down

Growing momentum

Before the final fall

Disappearing from sight

Like a coin in a spiral collector


Control slipping through weakening fingers

Touched but no longer touching

Sounds close but everything far away

Taste tantalised

Spasm grips

Life ebbing

But for God


Divine presence coming

Day drawing nearer

Family of Christ gathering

Sight unveiled

Glory

*"And those whose journey now I is hard*

*Whose hope is burning low*

*Who tread the rocky path of life*

*With painful steps and slow*

*O listen to the news of love*

*Which makes the heaven ring*

*O rest beside the weary road*

*And hear the angels sing*

*And still the days are hastening on*

*By prophets seen of old*

*Towards the fullness of the time*

*When comes the age foretold*

*The earth and heaven renewed shall see*

*The Prince of Peace their king."*[4]

---

[4] 'It came upon a midnight clear', EH Sears, 1849

# Weddings

## **Wedding in the Odenwald**

Gathering smiles
A century of friendship and kin
For this day of union
Under the simple wooden vaulted ceiling of hill top kirche
Standing proudly over its Odenwald village.

From far and wide friendship and invitation drew them there
To celebrate the long-held dreams of bride and groom
Coming together in answered prayers
In this joyful assembly
Decades of life's stories passed.

Pain of waiting forgotten, eyes meet
Ears alert to their exchange of vows
Covenant sealed with golden rings
And prayers of blessing.

Voices raised in praise
Held aloft by the sound of bow on string
Resounding in hearts warmed
By love's hope-filled longings.

Deep blue the sky
A palette of promise for days ahead
Red tumbling roofs below
Like the interconnecting of global chatter
Finding a common language of embrace.

Canopy of green floating on warm breeze
Lifting to heights above
For a wedding banquet prepared
To crown the day in schloss walls
A lasting foretaste of a coming Kingdom.

## Sunderland Wedding

Tears filled their eyes

Long-held hopes in promise

Eyes meeting over clasped hands

Vows and promises made

Quivering lips declare, I will, I do

Unconditional love we'll give

Rings exchanged

A seal upon their hearts

A crown upon their heads

Trembling hands relax

Glorious smiles break out

Joy floods the room

In Christ alone they sing

Praises lifted high.

# Alberta Wedding

Farmstead, forest camp
Community hall buzzing with creative activity
Friends and family preparing

Cake-baking in Airbnb
Subways sliced and filled
rum balls rolled, muffins iced

Sunrise spruce's welcome shade
A picnic for a burgeoning crowd
Hungry in expectation

Tears of joy and sorrow mingle
Hope filled surprise
A taste of heaven

Beneath the trees
Sun-rays dance
Music plays

His smile grows as
Up the hill she strides
His bridal beauty has arrived

Benches and bales mark out
A sacred space before a cross
For a solemn exchange

Eye to eye with quivering lip
I will I do, a covenant is sealed
Unending unconditional love

Hands held in tender grasp
Slender rings a symbol
Gold refined and pure

Heads bowed in prayer
On the breeze the Spirit floats
This sacred moment sealed

Smiles break out cheers rise
The couple embrace
With a kiss

*Desire for authenticity*

# Wedding in a Brew House[5]

No wasteful familiarity
Squeezing onto wooden benches
Joy over-spilling
Workshop with rising laughter
Doors flung open to sunlight
Standing room only

Irish music announces arrival
Couple stand before approving faces
Reaching hands and meeting eyes
Shared vows given in pledge
Holding words in thoughtful gaze
Touching hearts and minds

Notes dance from strings
Best-man passes rings for
Family and friends to bless
Golden bands exchanged
Names joined in mutuality
No loss of identity

---

[5] Woodside, Sheffield, S. Yorks

35

Cheers quiet as music cuts the air
The couples name announced
'The Turner van Keefs' embrace
Twirl and dance in delight
Twinkling lights overhead
Trestles laid with flowers and candles

Inspirational stories shared
Of self-giving love and compassion
Thai street food is served
Spontaneous lyrical Irish music plays
Trays of iced donut wedding cake
Sticky fingers and pints of ale

Lightning flashes across the city sky
River Don flows quietly by

# Retirement

## When the pace of life is changing

As retirement approaches

It's like feet dangling in the air with a parachute of faith

Facing free-fall without a ripcord

While all around others are planning ahead

As if with some certainty that life goes on

A clear landing mark within sight

Even cross-winds are a not a second thought nor is

Parachuting in tandem with a Master

Not gripping the ripcord handle if there were one

But letting go my breath with trusting exhilaration

Ground zero approaching faster than the eleventh hour

With the Master of the sky who holds my time in his hands.

*Twenty years of parish ministry in the church-by-the-river*
*brings me to retirement. With no future home on the horizon*
*I'm reminded of 'Israel' leaving Egypt with only a promise.*

## Longing for a place to call home

When belonging here is terminated
How I belong comes into sharp focus
When chain-making has slowed to a halt and
The dream of a new place to call home is suspended
The river behind but none will follow
A wilderness wandering with cloud and fire
To some faraway place of hope
With my closest and dearest holding unbelonging
While longing to belong again
Laying down a public role for anonymity

A draw-string of constriction or freedom's release
When belonging remembers its true home long-given
With the welcome of the Father's house then
His presence on the journey through the sea of uncertainty
And parched places, of manna given will reveal
The Promise-Keeper, His divine links secure
To provide a place which we'll call home
Whenever and wherever,
While all along belonging in the Father's home.

## Loss and Gain

Leaving behind and looking forward

Changing perspective in time and space

Putting down the weight of loss

Loss in fading beauty and vision

Loss of place and belonging

Loss of familiar smiles and ease of being

Loss transformed by redemptive faith

Holding the reality of new creation

New strength, clear vision, belonging

The gain of perfection in all things made new

Finding hope in a future glory

Leaving behind and looking forward

The gift of a new home - Peacehaven

At the last minute signed and sealed

Facing south in glorious sun

A place flowing with crystal chalk streams

Friendly neighbours call bearing welcome gifts

February's blue skies hint of gain beyond expectation

# *Faith*

## I AM you made me

I AM you made me to be me
I am a work begun
Becoming more alive
Awaiting the fullest sense of being
To know as I am fully known

Nature's notes surround me
Birds and bees, the rustle of leaves
A gentle breeze touches my face
As grasses dance in summer's sun

I AM you gave me and gave again
Creation to delight in and endless you to find
Work to do and rest to find and play
Not to control or be controlled, to define or be defined
But endless possibilities to find
As myriad colours from light are poured

I AM you are that Light which lightens up my soul
To become on endless day a beam of light for you.

*When getting tired of pastoral matters and wanting to cross the finish tape.*

## Running the Race

The field is not ploughed unless yoked with Jesus
The scattered seed only grows when he sends rain
The sheep are not fed without quiet waters and fresh green grass
Sleep is restless unless the Shepherd guards the fold

The fish are not caught until the net is cast on the other side
Hunger is not satisfied until bread is broken
Thirst is not quenched until living water satisfies
Without a soft heart peace can not be found
Without a quiet spirit joy will fly
Without humility wisdom evades

The race is not over until Christ calls us home
So breathe in the breath of God
Fill your lungs with his praise
Open your hands to receive his grace
And your eyes to behold his beauty.

*Trust in the Lord with all your heart, lean not on your own understanding; In all your ways acknowledge him and he will direct your paths. Proverbs 3:5-6*

## Holy One

He came not to be served but to serve

The one who made us came to serve

He humbled himself to serve

He whose sandals we are not worthy to untie

He came to serve

He invites us to follow

He doesn't demand but freely offers

He offers to carry our burdens with us

He calls us to lay down our lives

He offers the way of a cross

He promises life in him

He asks us to serve one another

He shows us how

He asks us to love one another

He shows us how

He asks us to give and not count the cost

He shows us how

We question self-giving with false motives

We question sacrificial love as it reveals our guilt

We question Christ-family love as an ideal but not a reality

We think the Kingdom of God is coming when it's among us now

We think our eyes are open when we still walk in the dark

We think first of ourselves and not of others

We behave as if this is all there is so

We don't truly rest or give sacrificially

We fill our days, hold tight to time and what's mine and miss

The delight of serving one another

He is the Holy One who invites us to be holy too

# Faith in the face of MND

For those moments you escaped the confines of your body

Smiles spread across your face, eyes alight listening

Humour a relief from relentless decline

Whispered words of grace you spoke

While struggling to breathe

The pain of loss wrenching body

But your faith-filled soul alive

Alive to learning you embrace His promises

The uninvited inhibitor stealing life piecemeal

Cannot quell the growing seeds of faith standing tall

The air concentrated not by oxygen but *ruach*[6]

Giving hope to certainty of promise

Over this life's horizon.

---

[6] *Ruach*, Hebrew for the breath of God's Life

# Ekklesia

*Reflecting on my encounters with Deaf Church and hearing loss in the hearing church.*

## Pardon me

The beauty of sound evades me, it's not all music to my ears
Noise begins to disturb what I once took for granted
Straining forward to listen to my fellow diner in College halls
A feeling of isolation creeps into my being

I watch my Deaf friends signing and full of smiles
Knowing their smiles hide so much of their own pain
Now I find myself between hearing, disturbing noise and silence
Noticing now what I hadn't heard before

Free from the city of noise
Appreciating the wonder of sounds all around
In the stillness of an ending day, when noise is quieted
I hear again as creation offers its single notes of praise.

The beauty of hearing, once taken for granted, fades
Stopping now to listen to the voice of the Spirit
I hear in the stillness once quelled by busy-ness
Voices of wisdom, grace and mercy resounding in the silence

The voice of God's heart is a beautiful sound
In this in-between as I listen again to
The signs of hands, the look on faces, and radiant eyes
Receiving the good news of the sound of heaven

Walls of separation will fall and the gift of being one in Christ
Expressed in the pure sounds of praise
The beauty of sound and light our new habitation
Resounding in all hearts and ears

*It's the 820th night since Night Prayer started on Zoom. On any typical evening those gathering are from their 60s to 90s. Some attend every night from their homes near or far.*

## Night Prayer

I open the Psalm, awaken my computer and light a candle
Evening light fades and thoughts turn to rest
Before my eyes the faithful-ones gather
In our shared virtual chapel
Waves and smiles are exchanged,
stillness descends as music plays

The eternal God is our refuge
And underneath are the everlasting arms
The psalmist's words touch our hearts, hope is strengthened
Holding our world, our loved ones and our pain
We give the weight on our hearts to the Father's love
His mercy and the shelter of his peace

The promise of the Kingdom coming in words of Scripture
Surrounds us like a warm duvet as we commend ourselves
To the shelter of his wings receiving again the Aaronic blessing
As music plays and fades we are thankful
For the moonrise and star shine, the beauty of the universe
And the little we can add to the Kingdom of the Son.

*Sunday intercessions included a courageous naming of truth*
*but some thought the words judgemental and lacking in grace,*
*while some praised, others gave a lamentful 'Amen'*

## Truth and Justice Meet

When truth is wedged in voice raised and finger pointing
Grace flees
The gentle dove-of-the-Spirit's wings uplift and fly
Circling around searching a place to alight

Humility holds the unanswerable mercy of our Creator
Whose cross was raised and forgiveness flowed red
Not a standard on a pole, but tears shed over us
Bearing the pain of all our brokenness and shame

When clothed in righteousness, by redeeming grace
None will be lost, not one
By love only will love be revealed
Soft and tender-hearted strength
That bears the injustice of indignant voices

To become nothing, that Christ may be our all
And the dove-of-the-Spirit find in us a home.
But prompting Spirit stirred
The one whose voice was raised
Struggles to convey, the sorrow in his heart

For the lost

The lost saints of the persecuted Church

The lost lives of those unborn

The lost blessings of not living by God's commands

His concern for the Shepherds of new Israel

Leading flocks to danger

He grips the lectern lest he fall

With raised and trembling voice he speaks

Will we, with quiet weeping,

Cease from our own pointed words

To find healing for our brokenness

And freedom from our shame

To allow the quiet voice-of-the-Spirit to lead us

And the dove-of-the-Spirit find in us a home?

*Should we expect always to be soothed by the Good Shepherd and not sometimes disturbed by our encounter with a Holy God?*

# Nature

# Cambridgeshire Country Garden

In a country garden the day is ending

Sunlight filters through dancing leaves
Robins click, daisies float, magpies chatter
Pigeons wings uplift for long glide
Through boughs canopied in green

The cooing of doves, trill of blackbirds
Swifts sailing black against high fading blue
Settling hush after a summer's day
Silver moon rising in Eastern sky

As darkness merges detail into shape
And colour evaporates into shadows
Birds' roosting song fills cool fresh air
The sun has slipped from sight
The day draws into night.

# Swallows

Carefree at nature's call - graceful

Wheeling the wind - aerobatic splendour

Tracing arcs on water - sipping in flight

Feasting on insects - invisible against the blue

Harmony of swallows soar

Flittering to rest in rows

Preening feathers before take-off

Chirping calls

## Sounds of Life

I hear its cry and look to see a kite's graceful wings riding high
the fenland air currents, its v-shaped tail twisting as it turns
in tight circles before vanishing from sight as if into thin air.

Nearer still robins click, their short flights from bush to shrub
distracting me from its warm clutch in nearby hedge.
Silent steps of muntjac deer and a rustle of leaves as it melds
through hawthorn and hazel perfectly camouflaged only to
awake me with its barking in dead of night.

Another day another place through glass doors I enter
an endless beat to which no one listens.  The clink of cups
fresh-washed, the clang of saucepan lids. The call of a name,
the thud of portafilter on knock box, a cacophony.

High above the Rhine skylarks sing while below a strumming
diesel train threads its way through tumbled towns, a sudden
gust of wind slices the hillside vines, awakening laughter.
Rustling paper in the boulangerie, deep rumbling chatter
of older men over hot coffee, tables filling, eyes searching for
sun or shade.

# Yorkshire

## North Yorkshire

Grey skies reaching to the horizon

Meadows give way to moor

Goods-train steady on incline

Copses of stunted trees

Sheep heads down while birds of prey

Glide and hover on the wind

Summit cresting view unfolds

Towards the east clouds break

Promise of a brighter day

Cattlegrid rumble then

Long steep descent river running

Scattered farms and barns

Estate gates welcome

Specimen trees stand tall

Shading antlered deer

Cloud skipping breeze

Sunbeams dance on ancient stone

Clinging to former glories

On the valley floor we stand

Before the ruined splendour

Jackdaws call, squirrels scamper

River raises its voice

Tracery reaching skyward

Once glazed, frames nature

Centuries have passed

Wooded dale rustles

Long gone the timber rood, roof and floors

The glories of bishops and kings have dimmed

Their place no longer in memory

Their names forever on the hand of God

# Riding Steam on the Embsay-Bolton Line

Thro' patch-worked hills
Stone-walled fields
Sheep grazing

Track-side flowers
Dance to passing train
Billowing smoke

Clanking memories
From bygone years
Steam whistles

Light-long summer day
Grey-skied mizzle
Green provides

Track tracing beck
How, Holywell, Lillands and Ings
Together flowing

Uncoupling clanks
Liberated engine
Traversing points returns

Carriage doors clang
Whistle blows
Chuffing takes strain

Reaching thro' open windows
Doors fling back
Passengers disembark

## Yorkshire Dales

Through stone-walled lanes
rolling and rising with cloud
rain softly falling
on verdant meadow
livestock grazing
to Malham, beck and tarn

Gurgling, swirling, rushing, surging
gill and beck under stone bridges
humpback and clapper, flowing
too fast for kingfisher or dipper
raising the stream gate
ford impassable

Meadowsweet and creeping thistle
colours glory in gusting wind with
yellow bedstraw, great willow herb
meadow crane's bill and wild angelica
the leaping water of Janet's Foss
dancing in Gardale Beck

Grey-stoned barns, sentinels of centuries

refuges in storm and home to owls

hunker in field's corner

limestone scars on hill and in dale

sanctuary for small mammals

kite and buzzard soaring high on gilded wing


Lungs filled with fresh breeze

and flora's aromatic air

feet following down stream

flow in fading evening light

cottage awaiting to give its rest

after the blessing of nature's gift.

## One The Bailey, Skipton

Surrounded by ancient stone

Glimpsing the castle gate and church

Tiny windows giving way to daylight

Thick walls resisting penetration

Disconnection from the internet

Giving peace and space in

Skipton cottage dwelling

Cascading green on towering walls

Surrounding bailey courtyard

A working space of bygone years

Through stone-arched gates

A parking place for cars

Moss now where feet once trod and besom brushed

Aside Skipton cottage dwelling

# Europe

# Heidelberg, Germany

Streets filled with chatter
Cobbles giving back clatter
To passing cars
Silent the River Neckar flows
Surrendering its power to control

Barges slipping their cargo beneath
Ancient gated bridge whose portcullis
Once held back the flow of men
White its round towers
Reach up with black onion domes.

Remains of schloss clinging to days long gone
While musicians practice the music of Bach
Fresher than the day it was written
Bells resound across the valley

Trees take high ground as the hills constrain our path
But the voices of the Evangelische Kirche
Will rise in choral harmony to make
A festival of praise.

## Neuchatel, Switzerland

Cobbled streets climbing
Culvert flowing down
Flags fluttering in canton colours
Mediaeval church and schloss over-looking town
Farel lifting high God's Word
Before the great west door
Embellished with bronze branches acorns bearing
No mighty oaks in sight
Three wolves prowling
Deep blue nave ceiling with bright
Stars shining down
No sign of today's faithful ones
This monument of past glories
Whose stones cry aloud His praise
For those with ears to hear.

# Canada

*All in a day's adventure with two nonagenarians;*
*from Agassiz to Nanaimo and back*

## Destination: Vancouver Island

The smell of smoke from forest fires in the air
Mountains rising from valley floor
The mighty Fraser flowing by
Leading west to the Pacific shore

Horseshoe Bay and Nanaimo ferry
Sun rising, coastal wind blowing
Brightening the mountains green
Stepping aboard we sit gazing to Bowen Island

Calm sea and big skies breaking blue
Dock receding from view
Bowen grows in closer sail
Before majestic Rockies rise

West on the Strait of Georgia
Past Gabriola Island into Departure Bay
A welcome hand as we step ashore
Blood is thicker than water

**Return voyage: day is ending**

Port-holes in the clouds
Releasing pools of silverlight
Dancing on the sea

Darkening profile of mountains
In setting sun colours
Slate-grey sea

Dreamy thoughts of what might be
A future in an island home
Head sinking into much needed sleep

*A road trip west of Rocky Mountain House, Alberta, into Banff National Park.*

## Rocky Mountains

Rising in grandeur through vision

Shortened by forest fires' haze

Rocky Mountains reaching skyward

Beyond the reach of spruce and larch

Milky blue waters of glacier-fed lakes

Spilling over rocks, tumbling down

Through forests alive with fauna

Chipmunks scampering, chickadee flitting

Creek growing, twisting, turning

Beaver building, wild horses grazing

Not a grizzly in sight…

Lightning flash, grey clouds looming

Rain falling, hail forming

Carpeting lumber trail in gleaming white

Sun breaking through, vision clearing

Skyline clear against heaven's blue

Forest giving way to pasture and field

Mountain turns ceasing

Range roads reaching as far as sight

Sun setting, coyote calling

Day ending in golden light.

## Alberta Acreage

Spruce standing tall surrounds

Through shimmering poplar leaves

Beaver-dammed creek glinting below

Hawk calling from blue skies

Mating dragon flies in flight

Summer sun warming the earth

Squirrels calling, neighbour mowing

Cattle grazing, pump jack nodding

Soft stillness of nature's enfolding

Alberta acreage

# California

## Pacific Shore

Ocean giving voice in ceaseless waves

Hopeful surfer bobbing

Palms reaching one hundred feet

Amtrak fringing sand with steel

Yellow beach flag fluttering

Life Guard lookout number five

Listed prohibitions

Small children skipping playful waves

White surf fizzing into sand

Boards beached and towels spread

Bronzed bodies covered against the wind

Klaxon sounding, barrier closing

Seven twenty for San Diego

Islands profiled against golden skies

Warm lighted Pacific Shore

# San Clemente

Mottled white and blue skies
Light breeze and gentle waves
On the Pacific shore
Slender palms reaching
Pan tile roofs climbing
Car-lined streets rising
San Clemente

Wooden pier, red life-guard buggy
Tannoy'd warning "leave the water"
Amtrak dividing beach and town
Four-wheeled mustang gliding
Quiet hum of hybrid power
Rubber on road
San Clemente

Umbrella'd ice-cooled drinks
Pooch on lead, under arm or bag
Four neon paw shoes
Half-price surfers' outlet
No waves in sight
Aromatherapy or CBD
San Clemente

## Laguna Beach - Colors

| | |
|---|---|
| Golden sand, crystal waters | turquoise |
| Clear western horizon sky | blue |
| Heisler Park flowers dusty | pink |
| Ice cream curled with beans | coffee |
| Gull gliding onshore wind | white |
| Headland scrub salt rusty | brown |
| Evening sun wind-dusted water | silver |
| Parking meter counting down | grey |
| Pacific coast highway stop | red |

# Queensland

*Having read a little about the 'Gruen effect' and encountering*
*a vastly expanded shopping mall in Maroochydore, QLD.*

## When life is complicated - the Gruen Effect

Collaborators confuse my mind

Separating the rhythms of nature from its gift to me

Darkness wrapped in LED light loosed me from time

Random moving like a robotic mower

I gather what I do not need

Convinced that I am forever young

Age catches up, time has flown

Stepping out and into daylight

Life is simpler, disconnected from

The digitally manipulated world

The gift of nature awaits rediscovery

The greens of earth and blues of sky

The sights and sounds of day and night

The beauty of youth and the grace of age

*Looking out across the Mooloolah River, Point Cartwright,*
*QLD, on Armistice Sunday*

## The View has Changed

Remember when we were here before

Looking out across the river

Flowing with eternal purpose towards the sea

And now, the trees have grown

A curtain of green drawn across our gaze

Glimpses threading through, memories of what was

Looking around this Armistice

The older men still look back to younger days

Some things never change

The brevity of life held in an ocean of souls

Calling from beyond a declaration of peace

Surpassing our feeble will

The One changeless giver of life

Looking forward from where we were before

Calling into being a more glorious view

*After retiring a house was providentially provided days before we left for Queensland.*

## Letting Go

Between two worlds I sit, gazing out to sea

A pause between one place and another

The rhythms of worship and duties to perform

Holding hope for others to grasp and pointing to the Light

Give way to packing boxes and letting go

Down-sizing and reprioritising to find new focus

Before settling to new purpose and adventure

An alien world of retirement to befriend

Bringing long-held dreams to birth

Every moment an opportunity for wisdom's creative grace

Between two worlds I reflect

Like blue skies in wind chopped waters

Longing for the stillness of azure blue

Crystal clarity settled out of patient being

Learning new rhythms of worship in elders' days.

# World

*Psalm 119 is written in eight verse sections following the Hebrew Alef-Beit. Alef represents: God, Word, One, First. Written in the early days of the Covid pandemic.*

## Alef

1. A viral epidemic in China gave no fear as we looked on. The media message was control - man's science is king after all.

2. Young Wuhan doctor raises the alarm but is silenced in viral death. Threat is denied chaos explodes.

3. China locks its city and in days builds a mega hospital, conflicting words fill the press as the virus spreads.

4. Flights are grounded, borders close and the skies fall silent in splendrous blue.

5. Nature reclaims the heavens as pollution falls, birds singing in clear air as breathless patients fight.

6. Traffic comes to a stop, roads silenced. Peace descends as people retreat to lockdown homes.

7. Words of hope are rare as a pandemic grips the wide-world. What end will this beginning have?

8. God the Alpha and Omega, the Alef-Beit, you are One. You spoke your word first, you alone are King.

*Beit is the place of God's dwelling or home.*

## Beit

Lockdown One

1. Confined to work and play at home
   Socially distanced time out to get essentials

2. Churches closed to large congregations
   Inviting God to dwell with us at home

Lockdown Two

3. Blessed or cursed by being family together
   Reclaiming the house as home

4. Decluttering and making the most of our space
   Saving time on travel - gaining hours in the day

Lockdown Three

5. Sharing screens for online work, school and play
   Struggling with internet speed and tensions rising

6. The sun is shining, the summer warm
   Outdoor furniture sales boom

Lockdown …

7.  I've had enough of home.  Let me out
    Walking tramples every path

8.  Who's counting how many times a day?
    "Rules are made for breaking"

*Reflecting on stories heard during the day from hosts and friends of those without a home, and eighty asylum seekers holed up in a local hotel.*

## A Drought of Justice

There is a drought of justice

A dried riverbed of righteousness

The occasional cloud burst of compassion

Pools of indignation that soak away

Leaving precious children and mothers

Stranded by bureaucracy and prey to fear

A child's wave and smile

A first offering of hope

This green and pleasant land tantalisingly close

But out of reach

Self-righteous rejection of an invitation

To enter the land of the stranger

To inhabit his story.

When will our eyes meet to see reflected in the other

The image of Christ?

My breathe is caught, come Sovereign One

And once again set your people free

Set a table for us to eat together

A roof over us to rest

A canopy of stars to dance under

A new dawn's sun to shine…


*…I want to see a mighty flood of justice, an endless river of*
*righteous living.*         *Amos 5:24*

## Vision of the World

Wherever I look my vision of the world is bleak
A couple sit facing unknown days
Weakened by bleeding and a growing brain tumour
They dig deep knowing by faith they are carried by the
Everlasting Arms they face the reality of mortality

In full spectrum colour a war enters my home
Tanks trundle through deserted streets wrecking havoc
A terrorised family stare from my inbox
Fleeing the horrors of their massacred village
Loved-ones lost in Mozambican bush

The Fund of Tears calls for my response
Transient glimpses of life penetrate this brutal world
Soothing music gathers for Night Prayer
Under vibrant setting sun the promise of a new day
The smell of new-mown grass jars my senses against the pain

The senseless suffering of fear and loss of dreams
Where can I turn my gaze to regain some hope?
Pain permeates to the deepest and highest places
Hands once pierced reaching down to the depths of death
Hold the promise of the throne of heaven

A cup of water and a piece of bread in his Name
The cross-born blood once spilled will make alive
All are not lost and pain will be gone
Glory will come and vision filled with joyful light
Prophecy of terror healed, of hunger gone and loss made gain
Fulfilled

*The export of Ukraine's grain is blockaded at port, East Africa's poor endure famine, the bread basket of Europe the theatre of war.*

## Bread of Life

Golden fields wave the promise of tomorrow's bread

Silos full, port blockaded, today's ovens cold

Bread baskets of the poor are empty

Turkana's tribesman standing tall in defiance

Of hunger's pains, his children already laid in dust

Penetrating eyes frozen, resigned to injustice

Stare from The Times page.


No cloud the size of his hand, as promise in the skies above

Missiles rain down cluster bombs on Ukraine's farmers

Waiting for a break to harvest

Sorrow binds these men from far away

Expressionless madness grips the Devil's tool

Frozen heart defiant of truth

Can prayer turn his swords of fire into ploughshares of life[7]

Where is God's steadfast love when besieged by hunger?

Cries so weak mortal life doth finally cease.

---

[7] Isaiah 2

## Eco-disaster, the earth is warming

Clutching at plastic straws to take the focus away
Ocean's top predator, men in factory ship
Clutching at automobiles to take the focus away
Earth's biggest warmer, cattle farming factory

Dollar-fed get richer
Fin-fed are blind
Power-hungry are insatiable
Eco-charities take the focus away

The power of evil can only destroy
Sustainability a hopeless dream
Human words as worthless as a scarecrow in a cucumber field[8]

Earth groans in waiting[9]
For a divine word of recreation
Of life restored to fullness for
Bird and fish, beast and leaf.

---

[8] Jeremiah 10

[9] Romans 8:22-23

*After reading 'The Lost Words' and 'The Lost Spells' by Macfarlane and Morris while confined by two crutches and a raised chair, sitting with a limited view surrounded by fencing while just a few hundred metres from the ocean.*

## Word

Logos the name above all other names

Holder of hope in a tarnished world

Hands written with all names

None lost not one word

Looking intently with eyes and ears

I search for voices in stirring breeze

And, shifting shadow to focus

On words present and nature's gift

Flash of colour and passing sounds

Chirp, click, whistle and guffaw

Palms wave and rustle

Against billowing clouds of grey

Lost from view the ocean's waves

Whose distant sound I hear

Not lost but missing from my day

Like words missing from vocabulary

Each word or name not lost or forgotten

No less my finite being

Together waiting new creation's dawn

Not lost but fully known

Logos giver of life to all words

Logos dwelling in us and among us

Logos who searches for the lost

Until the one lost is found

## *End Note*

It didn't seem right to end this volume without acknowledging the world's pain and suffering. I do so with faith, even when that faith is standing on the edge and placing oneself in the hands of God.

In the face of global tragedy, letting go into the hands of God, is all one can do; to be humble to the extent of being a fool for Christ, with nothing to confidently speak of but His word alone. Trusting that the speaking God will speak again for all to hear, not in our timing or at our request, but in a *kairos* moment of his revelation.

I bring nothing but a desire for God's kingdom, an attentive waiting for His presence, and to give my heart and mind and soul.

To end this collection I reflect on a incident 40 years ago, from my time in London's most acute paediatric critical care facility, and on the tragedy of loss in Gaza today.

## er the Little Children

### don 1984

his cosmopolitan city

wering symbols of victory stand

attleships and rampant lions

Bronze stallions and spoils of conquest

Celebrating past victories on other shores

While London's streets are restless with fearful eyes

From every race and nation

An incendiary posted through the door

Rips fragile pseudo peace apart

For the family making home

Nine floors above this inferno in isolation we wait

Gowned, gloved and masked

To receive a precious child

Who this morning danced and played

On the edge of life she lies

Charred beyond belief

Innocence stolen while she skipped

To receive the letterbox gift

Her chestnut eyes now closed in morphine sleep

The odour of burnt flesh fills the air

Father's desolate eyes weep with pain

As his child's life fades away

If this is a city at peace, pity the one that is at war.

96

## Gaza 2024

Too thirsty for tears to stream down his dusty face
Shuddering breath of grief wrecks his being
As in his embrace life-less she lies
The one who this morning danced and played
All around the city falls
Innocence stolen while she skipped
This great injustice has a price
These little ones whose life is stolen
Should tear our hearts today
To stand in solidarity and share this father's pain

Israel's heart now hardened like a millstone
Sows in conscripts hearts seeds of despair
In the sea of judgement it will drown when
Answering to the Rock[10] who is greater
The One whose kingdom welcomes children[11]
A Father's heart is breaking too
While skin and language now divides
Joy comes in the eternal morning
When in counting we will see not one is lost
He who bore the world's pain gave his life for them
The only hope for fear's redemption
To love our neighbour as ourselves

---

[10] The LORD is the Rock of my salvation, 2 Samuel 22:47

[11] Matthew 19:14

Printed in Great Britain
by Amazon